igloo

This edition published in 2008 by Igloo Books Ltd
Cottage Farm, Sywell,
Northants, NN6 0BJ
www.igloo-books.com

Copyright © 2007 Igloo Books Ltd

ISBN: 978-1-84561-978-7

Illustrations by Martin Impey

Printed in China

My Book of Firsts

My name is Domanic William Amstutz

I was born on September 24, 2008

My first home

We lived here for …… years

My favorite room in the house
was ……………………………

photo

Address 310 Holly Hills
apt 209
………………………………………
………………………………………

My first bedroom

The color of my bedroom was
.....white.........................

The first picture on my wall was
of...your...feet...+...hands

My first favorite things

My first favorite toy

My first favorite TV show

....

My first favorite character

....

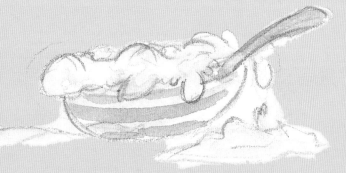

My first favorite food

....

....

My first favorite book

My first best friend ....

A photo of my best
friend and me

My first favorite outfit ....

The first time I...

...did a somersault I was ...... years old.

... caught my first ball I was ...... years old.

I was playing with ....

......rode a bike I was ...... years old

The color of the bike was ......

...went swimming I was ...... years old.

My firsts

I got my first tooth when I was .... years old.

My first trip to the dentist was when I was ...... years old.

I went with ....

My first haircut was when I was .... years old.

The first time I danced was with ....

My first pet was a ....

called ....

My first shoes were the color ....

The first time I...

. . . said a nursery rhyme I was ...... years old.

The rhyme was ......

....

....

....

...sang a song I was ...... years old.

The song was called ....

. . . said the alphabet, I was . . . . . . years old.

. . . wrote my name I was . . . . . . years old.

. . . counted to 10, I was

1 2 3 4 5 6 7 8 9 10

. . . . years old.

. . . knew the names of colors, I was . . . . . . years old.

My world

My first trip to the park was

when I was ..... years old.

I went on the

....

....

....

....

....

My first picnic was with

....

....

We ate ....

....

....

My first trip to the beach was
when I was . . . . . . years old.

We went to . . . .

. . . .

The first movie I saw was . . . .

My first time I ate in a restaurant

. . . .

. . . .

. . . .

. . . .

The restaurant was called

. . . .

The first time I...

... fed myself I was ......years old.

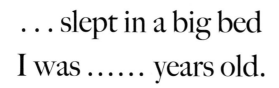

... slept in a big bed
I was ...... years old.

... got dressed by myself I wore

....

....

....

I was ...... years old.

. . . . drew a picture it was of a . . . . when I was . . . . years old.

My first trips

My first car ride was with

....

....

when I was ......years old.

My first bus trip was with

....

....

when I was ......years old.

My first train trip was

from ....

....

to ....

....

My first plane trip was to ....

My first boat ride was when I was .... years old.

My first day...

...at nursery school was on

. . . .

The nursery school was called

. . . .

. . . .

My favorite teacher's
name was

. . . .

. . . at school was on . . . .

I wore . . . .

The name of my school was . . . .

My favorite class was . . . .

My first Christmas

My first Christmas morning was at . . . .

My first Christmas present was . . . .

My first Christmas meal was . . . .

. . . .

I spent my first Christmas with . . . .

. . . .

My first Birthday

My first birthday
present was
. . . .
. . . .

My birthday guests
were . . . .
. . . .
. . . .
. . . .

I was . . . . tall

My first cake was made of . . . .

My second Birthday

My birthday cake was made of . . . .

My favorite

present was

. . . .

What I did

. . . .

. . . .

I was . . . . tall

My third Birthday

My birthday cake was made of . . . .

My favorite present was . . . .

What I did . . . .

I was . . . . tall

My fourth Birthday

My birthday cake was made of . . . .

My favorite

present was

. . . .

What I did

. . . .

. . . .

I was . . . . tall

My fifth Birthday

My birthday cake was made of . . . .

My favorite present was . . . .

What I did . . . .

I was . . . . tall